Stylish
NAPKINS

5-MINUTE IDEAS TO TRANSFORM YOUR TABLE

LABEENA ISHAQUE

NEW HOLLAND

For Naseem Akhtar

First published in 1998 by
New Holland (Publishers) Ltd
London • Cape Town • Sydney • Singapore

24 Nutford Place
London W1H 6DQ
United Kingdom

80 McKenzie Street
Cape Town 8001
South Africa

3/2 Aquatic Drive
Frenchs Forest, NSW 2086
Australia

ISBN 1 85368 809 6 (hb)
ISBN 1 85368 955 6 (pb)

Editor: Joanna Ryde
Designer: Behram Kapadia
Photographer: Janine Hosegood
Stylist: Labeena Ishaque
Managing Editor: Coral Walker

Reproduction by PICA Colour Separation, Singapore
Printed and bound in Malayisa by Times Offset (m) Sdn Bhd

Contents

Introduction · 4

General Hints and Tips · 6

Inspired by Nature · 8
Cockerel's Crest · 10
Swirl of Cream · 12
Scallop Fan · 14
Fleur de Lys · 16
Lotus Blossom · 18
Butterfly · 20
Peacock's Tail · 22
Hummingbird · 24

Tall Stories · 26
Asparagus · 28
Candlestick · 30
Tuxedo · 32
Nightlight · 34

Bishop's Mitre · 36
Cascade · 38
Palm Leaf · 40
Cravat · 42

Oriental Style · 44
Venus Fold · 46
Japanese Fold · 48
Tranquil Wave · 50
Pintuck Pocket · 52
Ocean Liner · 54
Envelope Pocket · 56
Bouquet · 58
Wimple · 60

Embellishments · 62

Acknowledgements · 64

INTRODUCTION

$\mathcal{N}$othing makes a dinner party, a romantic meal for two or an alfresco lunch more special than a beautifully laid table – apart from the company and the food, of course! A table laden with white bone china and crystal, or with earthenware bowls and chunky cutlery, can be given that extra touch with a lovingly designed napkin. Folding napkins need not be a time-consuming chore, but a quick and enjoyable experience with fantastic results. Whether it is a crisp linen cloth, a paper serviette or an organza extravaganza, napkins folded with care and consideration and placed at every table setting, will make your dinner companions feel special.

Napkins, or serviettes, have been used in Europe for many hundreds of years. Since the fifteenth century, they have been present at the most fashionable dinner tables of the royal courts, and used to clean hands and mouths after banquets. However, unlike today, they were not kept at the table, but near an oven, from where they were brought out at the end of a meal, still warm and, in many cases, lightly perfumed with a sprinkle of scent.

The napkin eventually became part of the table setting along with full dinner services and by the seventeenth century, folding napkins was viewed as something of an art. Napkins were folded into all kinds of shapes, from simple folds to intricately "sculpted" animal shapes like chickens and peacocks. It was thought to be positively rude to ruin these sumptuously folded napkins and fresh ones were supplied for the purposes of mouth and hand wiping.

From the early nineteenth century, napkins were being used at less aristocratic tables, as we can see from many paintings depicting diners with napkins tucked into their collars and tied around their necks.

Moving on into the Victorian age, "fancy" napkin folding became frowned upon in the more formal households. In 1881, Mrs. Beeton in her book on household management stated "fancy napkins are not fashionable", and that although there were several ways in which to present a napkin, elaborate designs were not in good taste and should, ideally, be neatly folded and placed on the plate.

But times change, and now a well-dressed table with creatively folded napkins can simply provide a perfect finishing touch.

GENERAL HINTS AND TIPS

*N*apkins, basically, are pieces of hemmed fabric provided during a meal to wipe hands and mouths. They are very often made from the same fabric as a tablecloth, the most popular fabrics being cotton damask and linen. Nowadays, however, there is a huge range of fabrics from which to choose, starting with practical and formal cloths, such as linen, through to more luxurious and decadent fabrics like organza. Sizes of napkins do vary, but the average size of a napkin is approximately 50 centimetres (20 inches) square. Do not be alarmed if your napkins are slightly rectangular or not quite symmetrical, as many mass-made napkins are not perfect, as I have often discovered when folding mine!

Do not worry if your folds are not exact, as your fellow diners won't be examining the squareness of their napkins, rather they will be admiring the overall shapes and how effectively they complement the table setting.

Alternatively, an inexpensive way to ensure that your napkins are absolutely square is to make your own. All this entails is taking a square piece of fabric and neatly hemming the edges, either with a sewing machine or by hand. By making your own, you will be sure your napkins are unique while also having the opportunity to be as outrageous or as conservative as you want in your choice of fabric.

To achieve a good crease or fold, you must starch your napkins. With traditional fabrics, soak them in starch and water before drying off. If, like me, you are not well-organised enough to remember to starch while you do the washing, use a spray starch, which gives exactly the same result as washing, and is far more convenient to use on small pieces of fabric such as napkins. Spray starch can be used on dry fabric, and sprayed on while ironing in the folds and creases.

The best way to create the folds, as shown in this book, is to fold your napkins on the ironing board, with your iron usually set on hot (but the setting, of course, can vary depending on the type of material being worked on) and on steam function. This allows you to fold and iron together, achieving a crisp and formal shape.

So, retrieve your napkins from the bottom drawer, where I'm sure they have been languishing since your wedding day, and enjoy folding!

INSPIRED BY NATURE

The folds in this section are influenced by birds, flowers and natural forms, with fan-like creases and shapes making intricate designs for more formal dinner settings.

COCKEREL'S CREST

A simple fold of a basic triangle is tweaked into an elegantly poised crest. This attractive napkin design is so versatile, it works well whatever the occasion.

Fold a napkin into quarters and press flat, then pull up one corner to meet the other to form a triangle shape.

Bring in two sides of the triangle so that they meet in the middle. The lower corners will protrude from the new triangle that has been made so tuck these underneath and press flat.

Fold the triangle in half so that the tucks meet each other inside. Finally, pull out each corner of the napkin that is visible from the centre to form the cockerel's crest.

SWIRL OF CREAM

Use a fine linen or organdie napkin to create a sumptuous, swirling design. The fine pleats are achieved by starching the napkin and pressing with a hot iron.

Lay the starched napkin out and fold one side in by 5 cm (1½ in). Press with a hot iron. Fold again at 5 cm (1½ in) and press.

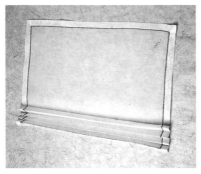

Repeat folding and pressing with the iron, until the entire napkin has accordion-like pleats throughout.

Hold the pleated napkin at one end and roll it into a swirl, letting the ends splay out around the swirl.

SCALLOP FAN

A very traditional, fan-shaped fold has been given a twist with an extra layer and folded-in corners to create a shape reminiscent of the shell patterns on the dinner service. Napkins with embellished edges can give this simple fold an added dimension, too.

Lay the napkin flat and bring the lower edge up to fold it so that it lies just beneath the top edge.

Bring the folded edge down again, so that it lies above the fold and then bring the top edge down to just above the lower edge and press firmly.

Starting from one side, accordion pleat along the length of the napkin. Pinch in the lower edge and fold in the corners to create a scallop-like shape.

FLEUR DE LYS

This is a traditional fold suitable for most napkins, apart from very flimsy ones. Once this fold has been mastered a number of variations can be achieved, such as the Bishop's Mitre (see page 36) and the Cravat (see page 42).

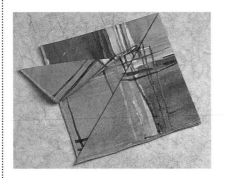

Fold the napkin in half to form a triangle, then fold in the two outer edges to meet in the middle with their free corners at the top.

Roll up the lower corner until it reaches the centre of the napkin.

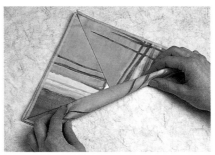

Taking the two outer edges, pull them around to the back and tuck one into the other. Fold the two free corners out.

LOTUS BLOSSOM

The napkin used here for this elegant shape is slightly rectangular, but it would equally suit a square napkin. To make it square, simply pull in the centre and press when the folds have been completed. With this type of fold, one can place the cutlery or a bread roll into the centre of the napkin.

 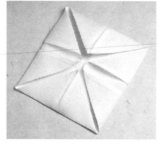

Fold the four corners of the napkin in towards the centre and press along the lines firmly, then turn the napkin over.

Fold the corners of the newlymade square in towards the centre again, pressing along the lines and turn over.

Taking the corners on this side, fold the corners in towards the centre and press, so that the corners now stand proud of the square like petals.

BUTTERFLY

*This fold works best with a lacy napkin or
one with detailed edging like a scallop, or
cutwork around the edges. The curled
parts of the top layer represent the wings of
the butterfly as it rests on the plate.*

Fold two sides in so that
they meet in the centre,
then fold the napkin in
half lengthways so that the
decorative edges are facing
outwards.

Mark the centre of this
rectangular shape and then
fold the two ends in
towards the middle and
then out again, so that the
lacy edges are on three
sides of the top layer.

Curl in the
top layers to
form two
conical shapes
at the top of
the napkin,
making them
meet at a
point at the
lower edge.

PEACOCK'S TAIL

This fan-shaped fold looks exactly like its namesake. It is free standing and extremely elegant, whether the napkin is made from a starched linen or a denim fabric as it is here.

Fold the napkin in half and then starting at one short end, proceed to accordion pleat it until you reach about half way down.

Fold the pleated short end in half, then at the opposite end, fold the complete napkin over at a forty-five degree angle, so that the bottom edge protrudes underneath.

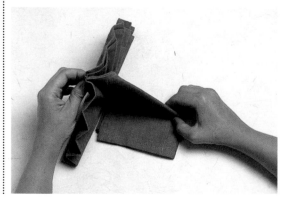

Stand the shape up on the support that has been created at the back of the fan, and the pleats will fan out by themselves.

HUMMINGBIRD

This particular fold works well on very fine or silky napkins, which show off the pleats to maximum effect. The tight pleats can be achieved with heavy starching and a hot iron, so that the finished effect is like the wing of a bird in flight.

Starting at one edge, finely accordion pleat along the napkin's length, pressing firmly as you work along it.

Make a knot at one end, leaving a short tail.

Finally, fan out the napkin's "wing" and place it on the dinner plate.

TALL STORIES

*The napkins in this chapter tend to be
upright and free standing, making them
suitable to stand alongside the place setting.*

ASPARAGUS

Fold and roll a napkin to create a crisp asparagus tip shape; this is the perfect napkin-fold for an informal supper party. Just lay the napkin alongside your china with the cutlery placed on top or next to it.

Lay the napkin out flat and fold two opposite sides in towards the centre so that they meet in the middle. Press with a hot iron.

Each corner of the napkin should now be facing the middle. Bring out each corner as far as it will go and again press flat with the hot iron.

Working vertically from the first folds, roll one side into the centre, making sure that the corners are poking out. Then repeat with the opposite side.

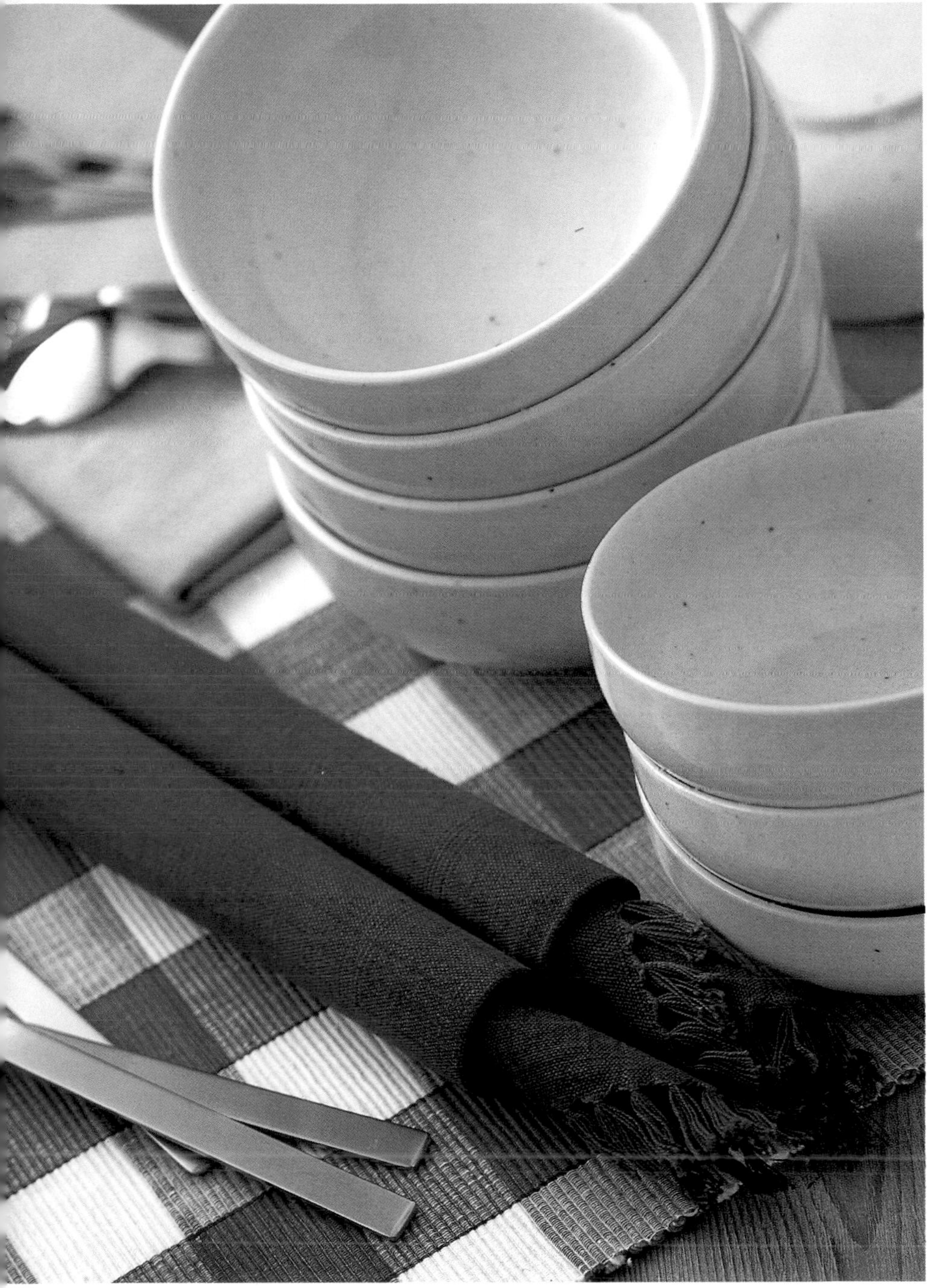

CANDLESTICK

These napkins look stunning when placed alongside very tall glasses. The fold, or "roll", is suitable for all kinds of fabrics, even the most flimsy, as the roll gives the napkin substance and allows it to stand without toppling over.

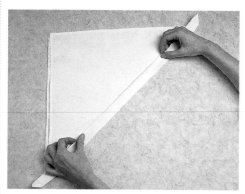

Fold the napkin diagonally into a triangle, then fold up the folded edge to make a cuff.

Turn the napkin over and proceed to roll it firmly and tightly from one side.

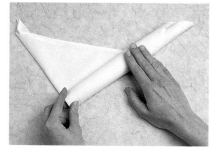

Tuck the free corner, made from the cuff, into the folded edge. This will keep the roll together and help it to stand upright.

TUXEDO

This fold looks rather like a dinner jacket, hence the name. It would be suitable for a formal dinner party and works best when used with a large stiff napkin, to ensure that it doesn't become too bulky because of the amount of folding involved.

Fold the napkin in half and then at one short end turn over a cuff of about 2.5 cm (1in), towards you. At the opposite end turn over another cuff, this time facing away from you.

With the cuffs facing away from yourself, bring in the corners to make a triangular top, with the cuffs forming a lapel-type shape. Do this with both ends.

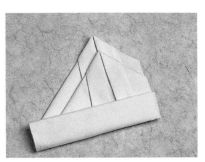

Fold the napkin so that the lapels lie one above the other, leaving a few centimetres (inches) between the tops. Fold up the lower edge to make a cuff and then tuck the two edges into the back.

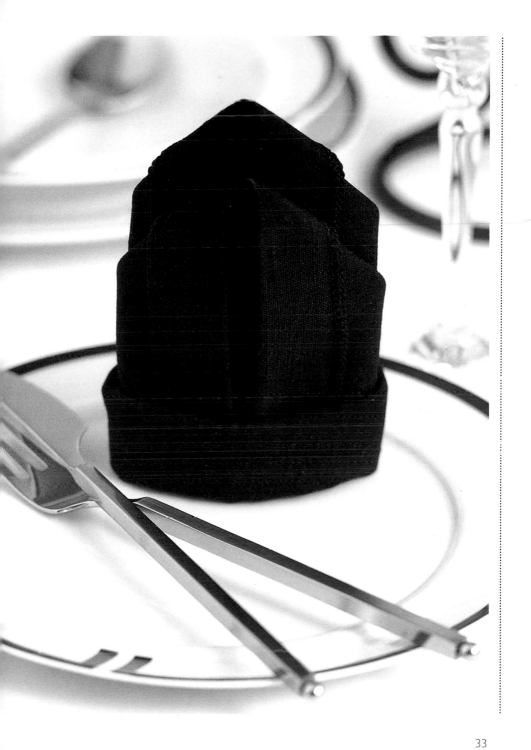

NIGHTLIGHT

This fold is similar to the candlestick, but a little less formal. The more starched the napkin is, the stiffer it will be and thus easier to roll evenly.

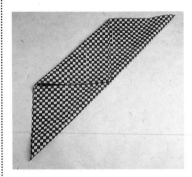

Fold the napkin in half diagonally to form a triangle and then pull down the top corner, so that it touches the lower edge.

Take one side of the napkin and fold it at right angles to the lower edge, so that the point is upright.

Proceed to roll the napkin, doing so tightly and firmly, then tuck the end into the roll at the bottom.

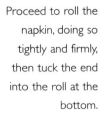

BISHOP'S MITRE

A very formal fold which is probably one of the most widely used at dinner parties and restaurants alike. This is best suited to a stiffly starched white damask napkin.

Fold the napkin in half diagonally, then bring up the corners so that the edges meet in the middle, to form a square.

Bring up the lower corner until it is about 2.5 cm (1 in) away from the top of the square, then pull the corner back on itself, so that it touches the lower edge.

Take the two outer corners and tuck one into the other at the back. Then take the two top protruding corners and tuck them into the cuff that has been made.

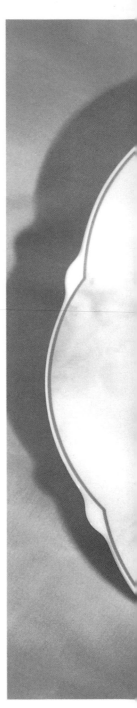

CASCADE

This delicate fold is meant to be placed in a glass, hence the very loose gathers, rather than folds. A luxurious fabric, such as this shot organza works well with this fold.

Fold the napkin in half diagonally to make a triangle.

Fold over the lower fold to create a wide cuff.

Starting at the centre, begin to gather the napkin into loose folds. Holding the lower edges of the folds, open out the gathers and then place it in a wine glass.

PALM LEAF

This beautiful, elegant fold forms a tall shape as the pleats are made diagonally across the napkin instead of the usual vertical pleats. The napkin should be thoroughly starched and stiff, so that it will stand upright without constantly toppling.

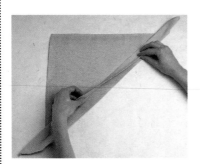

Fold the napkin in half diagonally, to form a triangle and begin to pleat from the widest part of the triangle.

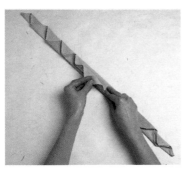

Proceed to pleat the napkin, accordion fashion all along the triangular shape, pressing each pleat firmly, with a hot iron as you do so. Complete the pleating when you reach the point of the triangle.

Fold the pleated napkin in half with the shortest side on the outside. Allow the longest parts of the napkin to meet and press firmly. The shortest end will act as a platform on which the fan will sit.

CRAVAT

This fold is very similar to the Bishop's Mitre, although the finishing touches give it a more informal look. The more relaxed finish means that many different kinds of napkins can be used for this fold.

Fold the napkin in half diagonally and then bring the outer corners togther to form a square.

Pull up the lower corner until it is almost half way up the square and then pull the corner back onto itself. Tuck one of the two outer corners into the other at the reverse.

Finally, pull out the loose corners at the top so that they stick out at the sides.

ORIENTAL STYLE

Origami – the Japanese art of paper folding – is the inspiration for these neat and precise napkin folds.

VENUS FOLD

This fold is so called as the diamond-shaped opening of the fold is similar to that of a venus flytrap. It is a suitable design for all kinds of napkins and can be pressed or not according to what type of effect you wish to achieve.

Fold the napkin in half diagonally, then fold the corners in so that the edges meet in the centre to form a square.

Turn the napkin over with the loose edges at the top. Turn the lower corner up to about half way up the square.

Turn the napkin over again and fold the left and right hand corners in to meet at an angle, then turn over.

JAPANESE FOLD

This angular design uses the decorative edges of the napkin as its focus. Napkins with stitched or detailed edges are ideal for this kind of fold. The pocket that is made can be used to slot in chopsticks or other cutlery.

Fold the napkin into thirds lengthways and then in thirds widthways, to create a small square.

Pull back the top layer so that it meets the lower corner, then pull the second layer vertically into the middle to make a tuck. Press firmly.

Take the two outer corners at each end of the first fold and tuck them around the back.

TRANQUIL WAVE

This very simple fold has a Japanese quality of tranquility about it. The design works particularly well on napkins with a border print, which will be highlighted by the gentle folds.

Fold the napkin into thirds across its length, with one of the bordered edges facing you.

Pull one side towards the centre of the rectangular shape, let the fold sit at the centre and the free end overlap at the edge; repeat at the other side.

Now turn the napkin over, so that the centre part of the napkin – with no border showing – is facing you. Flip over one folded side which will create two waves. Then just fold in another wave at one end.

PINTUCKED POCKET

This fold can hold cutlery or flowers in its pocket, but would look just as good alone, with suitably matching china.

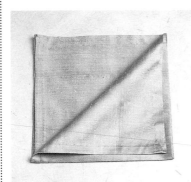

Fold the napkin in half and then in half again, to form a smaller square. Fold back the top layer at a forty-five degree angle to the square.

Fold back the next two layers carefully so that the points overlap each other.

Fold under the two side corners and press flat.

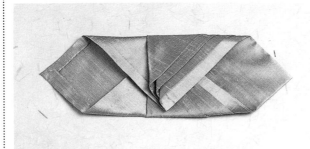

OCEAN LINER

This fold is so called for its likeness to a sea-going vessel and works particularly well with a checked napkin, as the symmetry of its shape can be reflected in the angle of the fold.

Fold the napkin into half and then half again to form a smaller square.

Using the free edges, tuck the top layer inside itself at a forty-five degree angle to the square end and press. Repeat with all the free edges, leaving a space of about 2.5 cm (1 in) in between each tuck.

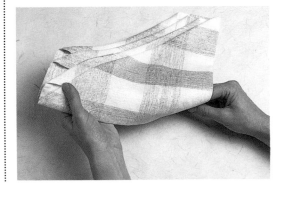

Finally, fold the square edge under and back out at the top to form the boat shape.

ENVELOPE POCKET

This symmetrical pocket shape design benefits from a check patterned napkin, as the lines in the pattern align with those of the fold.

Fold the napkin in half and then in half again, to form a square; then fold diagonally to make a triangle.

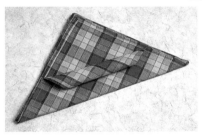

With the fold lying towards you, roll down the top layer, to form a cuff across the lower fold and press flat into place.

Pull each corner down towards the cuff, allowing a small distance in between each layer. Then take each outer corner of the napkin and pull towards the back to make an envelope shape.

BOUQUET

This bouquet-shaped fold can be used for holding cutlery or biscuits whilst drinking coffee. Napkins with patterned borders work really well with this type of fold as the pattern follows the edges of the design.

Fold the napkin in half and then in half again to form a square.

Fold the napkin diagonally along the square, almost in half, so that the top corners nearly meet.

Fold under the two sides so that the shape is triangular, and tuck one side into the other.

WIMPLE

The wimple is a fold which sits perfectly in a bowl with its ends protruding at the sides. We used a stiff, silk organza napkin to match the simple dinner service, but this design can be used on all napkins and is very easy to create.

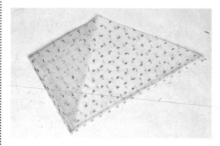

Fold the napkin diagonally to form a trangle, then fold up the two sides so that they meet in the middle to make a square.

Turn over onto the reverse, making sure that the free ends are facing you, then fold the napkin in half away from yourself, so that the free ends are now facing up.

Now, simply take the two outer corners, tuck one inside the other, allowing the two free ends to fall to the sides.

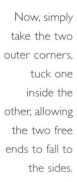

EMBELLISHMENTS

*M*ost napkins are simple squares of fabric. They are often quite plain and need no further embellishment. The print of the fabric is generally more than enough decoration, whether it is an overall pattern or a border. However, sometimes a little detail can give a napkin an extra something special, for example, the tasselled edges on the napkin used in the Asparagus napkin (page 28) or the embroidered details on the Scallop Fan (page 14). In fact, the napkin that was used for that design was a plain, shop-bought one, which I then decided to embellish by blanket-stitching around the edge in a toning embroidery silk. This works with complementary colours too, like the yellow cross stitching on the navy blue napkin used for the Japanese Fold (page 48).

One can also add details, such as sewing on a decorative braid or cord around the edge of a plain napkin. Sequins, beads and tassels can also be used to add further detail, depending on the type of fabric of which the napkins are

made. Sequins would not be suitable for a cotton napkin, but are for an organza one, for example, whereas folk art cross stitch motifs aren't appropriate for a silk fabric, but can be used on gingham. If you do want to embellish your napkins, lay out the threads and decorative pieces with the napkins and see how they look together before determining what will go where.

Napkin rings are not suitable for holding intricately folded napkins, but look effective with simple, rolled napkins. Another way to display a napkin in a ring is to pinch the centre of the napkin and pull it through the ring, for an informal, gathered look. There are so many different napkin rings to choose from that it can be hard to know which design is the right one. A common-sense rule to remember is to have plain rings with the more fancy napkins and leave elaborate rings for plainer napkins. However, it is very much a question of taste, so experiment and use that which you feel instinctively looks right.

ACKNOWLEDGEMENTS

The author would like to thank her friends and family for their help and encouragement: Martin Klejnowski, Brian Jellet, Jane Flockhart, Toby, Christopher, Sophie and Juliet Bawden.

The author and publishers would like to thank the following for their kind assistance in supplying props used in this book:

Narissa Mather
31 First Avenue
Kidsgrove
Stoke-on-Trent ST7 1DN
Tel: 01782 773083
(Silversmith)

Caroline Hudson
Studio Two
Cockpit Yard
Northington Street
London WC1N 2NP
Tel: 0171 209 0261
(Spotty ceramics)

Cargo
23 Market Place
Cirencester
Gloucestershire
GL7 2NX
Tel: 01285 652175
(Napkins and tablecloths)

Villeroy and Boch
Liberty plc
Regents Street
London W1R 6AH
Tel: 0171 734 1234
(China, glassware and cutlery)

Rosenthal China (London) Ltd
158 Regent Street
London W1R 5TA
Tel: 0171 437 1880
(China, glassware and cutlery)

Muji
26 Great Marlborough Street
London W1V 1HL
Tel: 0171 494 1197
(China, glassware and cutlery)

Dickins & Jones Ltd
224 Regents Street
London W1A 1DB
Tel: 0171 734 7070
(China, glassware and cutlery)